So Much More

Tanya Goyal

India | USA | UK

Copyright © Tanya Goyal
All Rights Reserved.

This book has been self-published with all reasonable efforts taken to make the material error-free by the author. No part of this book shall be used, reproduced in any manner whatsoever without written permission from the author, except in the case of brief quotations embodied in critical articles and reviews.

The Author of this book is solely responsible and liable for its content including but not limited to the views, representations, descriptions, statements, information, opinions, and references ["Content"]. The Content of this book shall not constitute or be construed or deemed to reflect the opinion or expression of the Publisher or Editor. Neither the Publisher nor Editor endorse or approve the Content of this book or guarantee the reliability, accuracy, or completeness of the Content published herein and do not make any representations or warranties of any kind, express or implied, including but not limited to the implied warranties of merchantability, fitness for a particular purpose.

The Publisher and Editor shall not be liable whatsoever...

Made with ❤ on the BookLeaf Publishing Platform
www.bookleafpub.in
www.bookleafpub.com

Dedication

To God,
for lighting my path.

To my mother and father,
whose love was the first poem I ever knew.

To my family and friends,
for holding space for every version of me.

To my younger self,
for never stopping believing in me.

To my readers,
thank you for choosing to pick up this book.
May good things always find you! <3

And to every soul I've crossed paths with,
thank you for walking me home.

Preface

So Much More began quietly, not as a book, but as a collection of thoughts that lingered longer than they should have. Some were born out of love, some from ache, and some from the stillness between both. Each poem is a fragment of something I once felt deeply but could not say out loud. Writing them became a way of listening to the world, to others, and to myself.

This book isn't about perfect conclusions or grand revelations. It's about small recognitions, the kind that arrive in the middle of a conversation, or while waiting for rain, or when silence feels heavier than sound. It is about the human tendency to search for meaning in moments that seem ordinary, and to find, somehow, that they are anything but.

Every poem here stands alone, yet together they trace a journey of learning, unlearning, longing, and quiet becoming. From the tenderness of love to the soft ache of loss, from self-doubt to rediscovery, these words hold reminders that we are never just one thing. We are always becoming. We are always *so much more.*

If this book finds you in a still moment, I hope it feels like a conversation, soft, honest, and familiar. I hope you see pieces of yourself in its pauses and possibilities. And I hope it reminds you, even gently, that there is more to you, and to this life, than what you can see right now.

Acknowledgements

This book would not exist without the quiet moments that whispered their stories to me, the small observations, the fleeting glances, and the joy and sorrow that live between breaths. The people who inspired these poems, those who stayed, those who left, and those who simply existed alongside me, your light, your shadows, and your truths have shaped the heart of this book.

To my readers, past, present, and future, thank you for holding space for these words. Every line was written with the hope that it might touch someone. This book is a map of a journey I hope we can share together, one poem at a time.

Thank you to BookLeaf Publishing for their #TheWriteAngle challenge, which became the stepping stone that encouraged me to voice my thoughts. To the gentleman from XLRI Jamshedpur, for his advice on the book title, without it, I might have named this book something fancy like *Soliloquies*.

To my parents, for loving me, supporting my dreams unconditionally, grounding me, and showing me how to be a better person. To my brothers, for their quiet, unwavering support. To Kashish and Manyata, my sunshines, my younger sisters, for their eternal trust, for reading my drafts, and for believing that my words hold the power to weave magic. To my friends Khushi, Kirti, and Divya, for being there through highs and lows, for thinking positively when I could not, and for believing in my caliber.

A special thanks to a dear friend. If someone had told me a year ago that I would write a book of my own, I would not have believed it. You made this possible. Thank you for always listening, for guiding me through darkness, for showing me I am so much more than I let myself believe, and for reminding me that there is still so much more I have to offer the world.

Every word in this book carries the presence of all of you. Thank you for being part of this journey. I am truly grateful.

1. Bodywash and Soap

I am lined up on shelves,
shining beneath warm light,
sleek among bottles
that look just like me.

While you,
you sit forgotten,
bare-backed at the edge of the sink,
shrinking quietly with each use.

I am used in handfuls,
wasting away in excess.
While you,
you fade with intention,
your shape thinning,
but never your purpose.

I change my scent with the seasons:
floral, fruity,
woody, and warm.
While you,
you stay honest and whole.
Just enough.

I am luster,
desire poured into a plastic cage.
While you,
you are calluses,
the mark of hands that have worked.

I was told
that if I smelled good
and looked pretty,
the world would always
make space for me.

And yet, I'm used
for the sake of foam,
spilled, forgotten,
replaced without pause.

While you, you endure.
You live in your own skin.
You are what you are.
You do not ask to be more.

Yet still,
when the faucet turns,
we both lather.
We both soften.
I coat the skin in scent,

you scrub away the day.

And when it ends,
we both dissolve.
You and I,
into water
that never once asked
who cost more.

2. Be my Pinocchio

Be my Pinocchio,
I'll ask, "*Do you like the stars?*"
"*No, I don't,*" you'll say.
Yet your nose will grow,
and I'll smile anyway.

Be my Pinocchio,
I'll ask, "*Do you like our talks?*"
"*No, not really,*" you'll say.
Yet your nose will stretch farther,
and I'll know you'll stay.

Be my Pinocchio,
I'll ask, "*Do you think of me?*"
"*No, my mind's away,*" you'll say.
Yet your nose will wander forward,
and I'll know your heart can't stray.

Be my Pinocchio,
I'll ask, "*Does your heart flutter for me?*"
"*No, not even slightly,*" you'll say.
Yet your nose keeps stretching,
because love can't hide away.

Be my Pinocchio,
I'll ask, "*Why does your nose grow so?*"
You'll smile, all wistful, then look away.
Yet I have seen it in your eyes
what your words betray.

3. Love Set in Keys

If you were a key upon the board,
be **Enter**,
where my words
would find their center.

Then I wouldn't worry,
I wouldn't feel lost,
when silence drapes
my thoughts in frost.

And I,
I'd be **Space**,
each pause
holding your gentle embrace.

If I were a key upon the board,
I'd be **Shift**,
lifting you close
through every rift.

And you,
you'd be **Backspace**,
erasing my fears,
my worries with grace.

If you were a key upon the board,
be **Control**,
steady when
life runs wild,
anchoring my soul.

And I,
I'd be **Escape**,
in highs, in lows,
your silent cape.

Together, *you and I*
would be **Caps Lock**,
two steady beats
in one endless tick-tock.

4. September Jasmine

It curls around rusted gates,
it spills from old gardens,
it peeks through small windows,
it climbs behind grey walls.

Its small white petals,
holding the hush of generations,
gathered at dawn.

It drapes over hair like a blessing,
it sits in bowls beside beds like protection.
It is worn, it is offered.
It is left behind, it is carried forward.

Its language written through scent, through gesture,
through the stillness it creates
inside whoever breathes it in.

And over time,
the nostalgia it holds begins to shift.
Once, it was a play between soft fingers & giggles,
petals pressed into strings like a secret.

Now, it arrives quieter,
a sudden breath caught in the chest,
a memory not of people,
but of presence.
A space where someone once was.
A time that once moved without urgency.
A time that cannot return,
but returns anyway
in scent alone.

What was once ordinary becomes sacred.
The same flower,
but now a ghost, a blessing, a home
unfolding in the air.

It is not just one story,
or perhaps just one,
retold in many lives.

It belongs to me, it belongs to you.
Or perhaps to no one.
Still, it is all of ours,
this quiet remembering.

5. Unnamed Butterflies

They arrived quietly,
wings brushed with a color
just past memory.

They hovered over hills
that remember how to bloom
only once in many seasons,
where violet light touches the ground
for a moment too brief
to be held.

Perhaps that's why they left.

Not out of fear,
but understanding.

Some things are too rare
to linger near
without losing them.
So they withdrew
before the petals fell,
before silence turned into absence.

Yet not everything that leaves is gone.

Traces remain
the hum in the air,
the memory in the soil,
the shape of movement where they once were.
Stillness holds presence.

The earth waits
as it always has.
It remembers the color,
the weight of wings.
And perhaps,
if the bloom holds longer than it should,
if the air opens just right,
they will return.

Not as they were,
not quite the same,
but close enough to recognize.

And maybe this time,
both bloom and flight will stay.
In quiet fields and in beating hearts.

6. Tracing You in my Palms

I don't know why I do this still,
but lately, when the night grows still,
I trace the lines across my hand,
like rivers winding through soft sand.

A map, a message, a secret sign,
a whispered thought you left in mine.
They're only lines, or so they seem,
yet in their curves, I start to dream.

Flesh and time have drawn them there,
creases born of fate we share.
And still, they feel like something more,
a letter slipped through some old door.

Not written by my hand, but you,
before I knew the soul in you.
Before your voice had touched my name,
before your fingers lit this flame.

Some part of you, before we began,
left a mark only time can scan,
a promise etched, a quiet vow,
a flame that burns even now.

It sounds so foolish when I speak,
yet in the silence, soft and meek,
when nothing pulls or pushes me,
a hidden truth begins to be.

I open my hands and close my eyes,
imagine you under the same wide skies.
*Wherever you are, are you doing it too,
palms unfolded, reaching through?*

*Are you by a window, watching rain,
or lying in darkness, dreaming again?
Do your fingers trace that hollow ache,
and feel the bond no time can shake?*

I swear you've lived in me, unseen,
longer than words could ever mean.
A soul I've known, though not yet met,
a love the stars will not forget.

Sometimes I whisper to the air,
"I'm waiting...," soft, a quiet prayer.
Not with yearning, not with need,
but patient faith, like planted seed.

No loud noise or bright display,
love like this walks a quieter way.
It comes like breath in tired lungs,
a melody hummed but never sung.

Who taught me to believe so deep,
that dreams can stir before we sleep?
That names are written skin to skin
long before our lives begin.

Yet still I do, I can't let go,
I trust the path I may not know.
I believe in you, not dreams or skies,
but in your hands, your heart, your eyes.

Not perfect, but warm and near,
a person who also feels me here.
Who wakes some mornings, heart half-lit,
not whole, but slowly knit.

I think when we meet, it won't be loud,
no thunderous sky, no dazzled crowd.
No lightning strike, no flash, no flame,
but something softer, without a name.

It will be calm, it will be slow,
like a sigh that's waited years to go.

I'll look at you, you'll look at me,
and no words spoken, we'll simply be.

We'll know we've held each other near,
in silent longing, year by year.
In palms, in breath, in hidden ways,
we've walked together through our days.

So I wait in patience, soft and clear,
holding hope that draws you near.
Each heartbeat tucks a prayer inside,
like a quiet wave, like a patient tide.

And when the world feels cold or tight,
or silence stretches too long at night,
I open my hand, trace what you wrote,
a secret message in flesh and note.

I read it again, though the letters are few,
and each time, it whispers,
soon... this love will come true.

7. In Someone's Shoes

I sit in the metro,
lost in my own thoughts,
avoiding eyes
that might unmask them.

So I lower my gaze,
to the shuffle of feet below,
each pair painting
a quiet story.

Some scuffed, some polished,
some worn, some new;
a gallery of steps,
crossing and diverging.

They speak without words,
each crease stitched with a tale,
each sole holding an echo.
The weight they carry,
the dreams they chase,
the miles behind,
the miles ahead.

Then my eyes return
to my own shoes.
Dusty canvas, quietly familiar.
Am I being observed too?

I wonder
if I slipped inside theirs,
or they walked inside mine,
*would the earth reshape
beneath us?*

But these soles, my discretion,
have felt my ground;
the grass, the gravel,
the stubborn stone.
*Perhaps the greener field
is where I already stand.*

I sigh.
***A hundred worlds pass in silence,
each apart,
yet bound
by the secret language of soles.***

8. Between Us, Rain

You watched the rain
through tinted glass,
while your fingers traced
a fleeting mass,
on fogged-up panes,
your face serene,
a quiet world
behind the screen.

I stood outside,
soaked in goodbye,
while you sat safe
as the car rolled dry.
I ran beneath
that sky so wide,
books wrapped tight,
with no place to hide.

That night I wrote,
your name withheld,
but in my chest
your memory dwelled.
You laughed when mud
made me fall,

outside the gate,
beyond the wall.

Years passed by,
you found new shoes,
and quiet halls
to chase your views.
Your smile on posters,
lit so bright,
your name in bold,
a shining light.
I passed as well,
but not the same,
not with grades,
but with the rain.

You posted clouds
to show your moods,
while I paid bills
and counted dues.
You wrote of monsoons,
deep and blue,
I wrote receipts,
with ink that grew.

Time made us taller,
but not near.

You walked in dry,
I awaited clear.
You chose the storms
that hearts pursue,
I faced the storms
of hunger too.

I waited outside
a glass tower tall,
resume soaked,
hope bound to fall.
Told to return
when skies were fair,
I swallowed doubt
and waited there.

You said the rain
recalled your love,
I heard it drip
on patched roofs above,
and silence thick
with a father's cough,
beneath a roof,
that kept heat off.

Still I wrote
on ticket backs,

on margins wide,
to mend the cracks.
Counting losses,
small defeats,
yet finding words
on crumpled sheets.

Now our hair is
streaked with grey,
our hands move slow
in gentle sway.
You speak of rain
as an old friend,
a beauty that
will never end.

I nod, though rain
has felt to me
a chill, a weight,
a quiet decree.
It made me small,
it made me wait,
a stranger still
outside your gate.

And today
the rain returned again.

You called it beauty,
I called it pain.
You drank it deep,
a poet's art,
while I held it still
inside my heart.

You said,
"*We've lived beneath*
the same wide sky."
I smiled,
but let the moment lie.
For the sky was ours,
but not the rain,
its cold decree
kept us apart in vain.

9. Lemon Soda

***Some friendships
are like lemon soda.***

No, not the polished kind
from shiny bottles in a fridge,
but the messy kind,
poured on the street,
under the slow-turning fan
of a corner shop.

In a glass that's lived many lives,
rim dusted with salt,
chili clinging to the edge
like stubborn memories.

They start with a fizz,
that sudden joy of finding
someone who laughs like you,
thinks like you,
feels just a little too much,
and doesn't hide it.

The first sip? Electric.
Cool relief on a hot,

unforgiving day.
You talk for hours
without checking the time,
share secrets like passing change,
make promises that feel
as endless as summer.

But lemon soda
is never just sweet.
Sometimes the lime hits too hard,
the salt catches in your throat,
and you wonder
if this mix was ever meant
to sit right.

Some days, your conversations go flat.
Replies get shorter,
pauses grow longer.

There are eye-rolls
instead of understanding,
silences that say
more than words ever could.

You disappoint each other,
say things you don't mean,
grow in different directions,

like vines climbing separate walls.

And yet, somehow,
you keep coming back.
Not every day,
but in the quiet moments,
when you're sipping chai alone,
or passing a familiar place,
or laughing at a joke
only they would get.
You remember.

You remember the fizz.
The firsts.
The fights.
The flavors that stayed.

Because even when the sweetness fades,
the memory holds.
Not all friendships are neat or fair.
Some are sharp, unpredictable,
spilled too fast,
or left unfinished.

But they mattered.

They taught you that love
can coexist with hurt,
that closeness doesn't
always mean comfort,
and that forgiveness
is a flavor too.

Some friendships are like lemon soda;
sweet, sour, salty, and real.
Not perfect,
but full of life.

And in the end,
you don't crave it
because it was flawless.
You crave it
because it made you *feel.*

10. Blessing from Pisa

Some people arrive
like summer rain,
in a manner
we can't explain.

They light us up,
then slip away,
we swear they were
meant to stay.

Some wander in
without a sound,
no thunder when
they come around.

But day by day,
they gently grow,
like roots beneath
where hearts don't show.

It's strange, the ones
we hold so tight
can vanish softly
in the night.

While those we never
thought would stay
remain beside us
day by day.

We question loss,
we curse the ache,
the promises
that had to break.

But even pain
can shape and mend,
each ending holds
a hidden end.

For every soul
that comes and goes
leaves something
time will soon disclose.

A lesson, a truth,
a spark, a scar,
a glimpse of who
we really are.

Some came to teach
us how to fall,
some stayed to show
we had it all.

And maybe that's
the gift they bring,
not always love,
but *a blessing,*
an awakening.

Not all light
is meant to stay,
but even stars
that fade away
once lit the skies
to help us
find our way.

11. Checkered Threads

Half joy, half pain,
half sunshine, half rain,
half tears, half laughter,
half order, half disaster.

Half bold, half shy,
half low, half high,
half quiet, half loud,
half lost in the crowd.

Half empty, half full,
half push, half pull,
half hope, half doubt,
half certain, half about.

Half logic, half whim,
half grin, half grim,
half courage, half fear,
half fleeing, half near.

Half truth, half lie,
half answer, half why,
half story, half song,
half right, half wrong.

Half clash, half blend,
half break, half mend,
half chaos, half peace,
half birth, half cease.

Half light, half dark,
half tender, half stark,
half tamed, half wild,
half calm, half riled.

Not one color, not one shade,
our emotions flow in their cascade.
We carry our flaws, we wear our scars,
we dream in fragments, we reach for stars.

You and I, we're a living enigma,
a contradiction, an oxymoron.
Two sides of the same coin,
residing within a single soul.
We're checkered threads,
walking each other home.

12. Cactus and Rose

I do not bloom
to draw a crowd,
I bloom alone
away from loud.
In quiet nights
without a light,
beyond the gaze,
beyond the sight.

Still, *I see you*
soft and bright,
bathed in warmth,
kissed by light.
You draw their praise
like summer rain,
while I endure
the drought, the strain.

Your roots are fed,
your petals wide,
your garden lush,
with none to hide.
And me? I cling
to barren ground,

where little grows
and less is found.

They love your red,
your velvet tone,
but fear the way
I stand alone.
They praise your bloom,
my spines they shun,
forgetting we both
reach for sun.

And sometimes,
if truth breaks through,
I ache inside,
I ache for you.
To be reached for,
free of fear,
to be called "*beautiful,*"
held near,
to be seen for
what is true,
not studied for
the thorns I grew.

So yes, some days,
a thought takes root,

its petals dark,
its stem like soot.
What if the sun
forgot your grace?
Would eyes then turn
to my small place?
Would I mean more
if you weren't there,
or just stand lone
in harsher air?

And in that moment,
I see you,
not from afar,
but clear and true.
How even petals,
soft and fair,
can hide the weight
of silent care.

The crowd that gathers
near your grace
soon fades when time
forgets your face.
And though you bloom
with colors wide,
your roots still shake

beneath your pride.

Behind your glow,
I sense the strain,
a quiet, well-concealed pain.
And then I see,
we both have scars,
just shaped by different
suns and stars.

My pain is silence,
cold and deep,
while yours performs,
yet cannot sleep.
If envy digs
too deep,
its thorns will turn
and make me bleed.
I'll twist with spite,
grow dark and thin,
and rot from somewhere
deep within.

But if I choose
a gentler view,
compassion for myself,
and you,

then something soft
begins to grow,
a peace I never
used to know.

You're not a rival
in my sky,
not one I must
outshine to try
and dim so I
can brighter be,
*you are a mirror
held to me.*
Another soul,
not free from strife,
just clothed in
different shades of life.

So I stay rooted,
firm and still,
with steady will,
against all ill.

**And when I bloom,
though none may see,
I'll know that it's enough
for me.**

Not to compete,
not to impress,
but just to live,
no more, no less.
Not seeking fame,
nor craving praise,
just growing in my
own *quiet* ways.

13. No Strings Attached

They tied strings to my hands
before my hands knew to reach,
to hold, or to fight.
Already looped tight,
in ribbons telling me to be nice.
This lace of lies,
asking me to be polite.

Pretty, delicate,
decorated with duty.
But heavy, these strings,
oh, so heavy.

They taught my fingers
to fold, not to point,
to hold teacups,
and never disappoint,
to wave, not to warn.
The creator of their very being,
still held with scorn.

They told me
quiet was beauty,
and obedience, a kind of grace.

They crowned silence
as though it were a halo,
and carved "*less*"
into the shape of my face.

They clapped and rejoiced
when I danced to their tune.
When I swallowed my "*no's*"
and lived in a cocoon.

I lived a script
written by hands not mine,
smiling on cue,
sitting still in a shrine.

They called it "*womanhood*"
but only if I stayed within
their definition.
They wrapped praises
in sweet premonition,
and kept wronging me
in what they called
an age-long tradition.

And so I bent.
I bent until my edges blurred.
In silence dressed,

but deeply stirred.
Until each nod, each bow,
each swallowed word
turned my voice into a whisper
I barely heard.

But somewhere,
in the hush between
who I was
and who I might be,
a flicker sparked,
a rebellion marked.

Questions rose softly:
What if I was made for more
than dancing on a bound floor?
What if being soft didn't make me weak,
but held a strength they'd never seek?
What if I was a storm before bloom,
not meant for a vase,
but to outgrow the room?
What if these strings weren't secure,
but chains in silk
I had to endure?

So I started,
I started to tug.

Gently, at first.
Then with ache, with hunger,
with raging thirst.

I tugged
until lace became rope,
and rope became chain.
I tugged them,
again and again.

And then I broke it.
I broke it
with shaking hands,
with tears falling
like broken strands.

I broke it.

And now,
I am no more their puppet,
no longer in their clutch.
I've changed,
they say I have become too much.
Too loud, too wild, too sure.

But I feel I've become pure.
Not pure as they mean,

but pure in presence,
in power,
in my very being.

Now, unstrung from those strings,
I dance to songs,
my own voice sings.
I know I was made to create,
to cradle,
to disarm.
To reach into fire
and still rise
with gold in my palm.

14. Still the Fairest, Always You

You used to stand
before the glass,
like meeting a friend
you knew would pass.
Chin held high,
no hint of doubt,
grace moving
from inside out.

You knew your worth,
it filled the air,
not just beauty,
something rare.
It didn't beg,
it didn't strive.
*It simply was
fully alive.*

I watched you.
Earrings danced in your hair.
Your bright smile
lightened the air.
You didn't walk,

you took command.
You entered rooms
and made a stand.

Now you pause.
Unsure. Withdrawn.
As if the mirror's
face has gone.
You glance,
then turn aside,
fingers searching for
where hopes may hide,
for something lost
you can't define.

I see it.
That quiet ache,
the words you speak:
"*I don't look the same today.*"
A sigh so soft,
a breath so deep.

But hear me. Fierce and true.
You are not skin, nor glass,
nor lines you trace,
nor shadows creeping slow.
You are more

than what the mirror shows.

You are the tale
still being told,
in earned laugh lines,
in courage bold,
in eyes that shine
through storm and rain,
in hands that hold
both love and pain.

The mirror is not
a judge, nor foe.
It sometimes cannot show
the truth beneath
its fragile face,
the strength
time cannot erase.

Mirror, mirror,
on the wall,
who's the fairest
one of all?

Still you.
Always you.
Not for looks,

but all you do.
For rising soft
yet unafraid,
worn but bright,
a light that stays.

To every woman
who doubts her face,
hold your worth
with quiet grace.

Beauty does not fade away,
it deepens, softens, finds its way.
Rooted in all
you've ever been.
Let the mirror see within.
Let *yourself* remember
once again.

15. Behind the Frame

Look close, don't just glance,
I am more than this still stance.

A smile that lingers, slow to part,
A secret safely held in heart.

Do you wonder what I'm thinking,
Or just see lashes softly blinking?

With silent laughter, soft and sly,
A teasing truth beneath the sky.

I am the pause you cannot break,
The breath you hold, the thrill you take.

A flicker caught within your sight,
A candle dancing in the night.

I see you leaning, searching near,
What is it that you wish to hear?

A whisper? A sigh? A hidden plea?
Or just the echo of mystery?

Behind these lashes, long and deep,
Are tales I've chosen not to keep.

Some desires are mine alone,
To cradle softly, all unknown.

I wear my grace like finest lace,
Dare you look beyond my face?

I am the silence in the room,
A whisper wrapped in faint perfume.

The glance that drifts, then withdraws,
Defying all your prying laws.

Lean closer, feel my quiet flame,
But never ask from where it came.

In stillness, I remain untamed,
A mystery neither caught nor claimed.

I am the woman in the frame,
Forever shifting, yet never the same.

16. A Full Circle or a Loop?

I walk the path, the same circle.
A loop etched into earth
by repetition and by habit.

It is a familiar walk.
A return to the same trees,
the same gravel,
the same subtle shift in morning air.
Nothing has changed, and yet
everything feels slightly new.

The golden hues of dawn
filter through branches in streaks and fragments.
They rest on leaves still glistening with dew,
on the curve of a petal just opening,
on the edge of a bench no one sits on.

Flowers scatter the path.
Some white, delicate like breath,
others bright yellow,
with the sun still folded inside them.

And in this soft encounter,
I feel a wordless pull.

And I want. God, I want to lift my arms wide,
to open my chest fully,
to let the beauty pass through me,
not just around me.

Yet my arms remain at my sides.
My body still,
held by the thought of being seen.
What if someone is watching?

So I continue to walk,
quiet & contained.

But the question lingers.
What if I truly absorb it all?
What if I let beauty in fully,
without filter, without fear?

And deeper still,
Who am I, truly?
When stripped of name, role, and memory?
When no one is watching,
no performance, no image to uphold?

The path continues to curve
and my thoughts continue to spiral.

Perhaps identity is not fixed.
Perhaps it is not a monument carved in stone,
but a shifting river changing its terrain.

Perhaps it is not owned, but borrowed.
Perhaps it is not discovered, but remembered
in moments like this.

Moments when the world opens
and something within opens with it.

The birds do not ask for names.
The light does not care who receives it.
The wind touches every face the same.

Yet still, I long to ask.
To whom do I belong?

Perhaps the answer is not a person,
not a nation,
not even a singular self.

Perhaps I belong not to anyone *but this. Only to this.*
This space between inhale and exhale,
between looking and being seen.

Perhaps I belong to the air
that moves in and out without permission,
to the dirt that holds the weight of bodies,
to the sky that has never stopped offering itself,
to the dust motes caught mid-air like tiny stars,
to the silence between leaves,
to the way light leans at dawn,
to the pulse in my wrist,
beating in time with something older than memory.

Perhaps I am not a solid thing,
but a flicker of presence.

So I continue to walk,
quietly holding the gesture
I long to make.

But inside, my hands are open.
Inside, I am letting it all in.

And that is enough.

17. Balloon Thoughts

I think we're all just balloons.
Not the shiny kind tied to birthday chairs,
but the quiet ones
that float up to the ceiling
and get forgotten after the cake is gone.

We start small.
Folded, waiting in a drawer,
some dusty corner of time,
with no idea what we'll become.

Then someone breathes into us.
Maybe it's love.
Maybe it's heartbreak.
Or childhood stories whispered at bedtime.
One breath after another,
lessons, guilt, kisses, small triumphs,
until we begin to take shape.

We puff up with dreams.
Stretch to hold hope.
Rise high. *So high*,
we think we'll never come down.

But the air never stays the same.
Sometimes life slips the string.
Sometimes we let go ourselves.

We float.
We drift.

We bump into ceilings, people, places
that don't feel like home.
We smile. Still full, still round,
but no one sees the tiny leak.
There's always a leak.
Always.

We grow lighter,
not the freeing kind,
more like something vital has slipped away.
We laugh a little less, a little softer
We don't bounce back so fast.
We wonder why we're tired
even after doing nothing at all.
It's strange, isn't it?

No one teaches us
how to deflate with grace,
how to release the air
we no longer need

without feeling like we've failed.

Maybe that's the point.
Maybe we're meant to change shape,
to lose what we once thought we needed.
To shrink, not into nothing,
but into something new.

Even a flat balloon
once knew how to fly.
Even in stillness,
it holds the memory
of floating.

And maybe that's enough.
To know we lived,
we rose,
we held so much inside us
and gave it room to breathe.

And maybe when we unbecome,
it's not the end.

Just the start
of something quieter,
something honest,
something human.

18. Crayon Confessions

I am a crayon.
Not the sharpest in the box,
not the brightest,
but I've colored enough pages
to know what matters.

When I was new,
I thought the goal
was to stay that way,
a perfect point, a clean wrapper.
Chosen first.

But over time,
I learned that being used
isn't the same
as being used up.

I've been part of quiet mornings
at kitchen tables,
held in small hands
drawing big dreams.
I've helped skies turn orange,
grass turn blue,
and hearts to believe

that nothing ever has to make sense.

Sometimes I stayed inside the lines.
Sometimes I didn't.
Both felt right,
in different ways.

I've been pressed too hard,
snapped once or twice,
sharpened roughly,
but I still draw.

I've watched others;
some more vivid,
some less worn
and I used to wonder
if I was fading too fast.

But now I see,
we all wear down eventually.
Not because we're broken,
but because
we've been part of something.

Every mark I've made,
every page I've touched,
it stays,

even if I don't.

*I may not look
the way I started,
but I've never been
more myself.*

There's something honest
about being a little dull,
a little peeled,
and still ready to color
whatever comes next.

*So no,
I'm not new anymore,
but I am still here.*

**And I still have
a little wax left
for something beautiful.**

19. Roll of Thumb

Thumbs keep moving,
but it's not just the thumb that rolls.
It's life slipping quietly
through glass screens and glowing scrolls.

We come seeking relief,
a laugh, a breath, a spark.
But the scroll gives us shadows,
and leaves our thoughts dark.

Curated smiles, perfect light,
stories trimmed to fit the frame.
Still, we compare ourselves
to faces that don't know our name.

Anxiety dressed in reels,
inadequacy dressed in views.
Self-doubt hiding softly
in the lives we didn't choose.

We call it a break,
but the break breaks us too.
Attention scattered in pieces
that no longer feel true.

We live to perform,
to pose, post and repeat.
Even joy and sorrow
are made to look neat.

And no one is truly alone
in this endless scroll.
A quiet ache for presence,
a longing beneath it all.

We've gained the world in pixels,
but lost the pulse of now.
And somewhere deep inside,
we're asking *how*.

How to sit without distraction,
to feel without a filter on,
to live the unedited moments
before they're gone?

Perhaps it starts with noticing,
a breath, a glance, a pause;
a shared awakening
to a deeper cause.

We are not the numbers,
the edits, or the view.
We are the breath between swipes,
the stillness breaking through.

Beneath the reels,
lies something surreal;
not perfect, not polished,
but fully human.
And real.

20. Dancing on Bubble Wrap

The world is thin as paper skin,
one breath away from breaking in.
Sometimes we'll lose, sometimes we'll win,
yet we'll stay through thick and thin.

You and me, hand in hand,
we'll dance on the bubble wrap,
laughing loud as the bubbles snap.

We'll chase the music no one hears,
beyond the noise, beyond the fears.
We'll entwine in dreams no distance sears,
across the hush of passing years.

You and me, hand in hand,
we'll dance on the bubble wrap,
laughing loud as the bubbles snap.

When silence wraps the world too tight,
we'll shout with joy, we'll claim the night.
We'll blaze a trail with borrowed light,
and turn the cracks to gold and bright.

You and me, hand in hand,

we'll dance on the bubble wrap,
laughing loud as the bubbles snap.

The ground may crack, the stars may fall,
the night may descend and shadows sprawl.
We may not catch each time we fall,
yet love will hold us through it all.

You and me, still hand in hand,
we'll dance on the bubble wrap,
laughing loud as the bubbles snap.

21. To You, Who Finds My Words

I've carried these words
like a parent with care,
not just in my hands,
but in breath everywhere.

In the quiet corners
no one could see,
they whispered softly
belonging to me.

Foolish, tender, desperate,
I held them tight,
hoping they'd bloom
in the darkness of night.

I fed them my sorrow,
my laughter, my tears,
the quiet, the stillness,
the weight of my fears.

I gave them the things
I couldn't say loud,
and in return,

they lifted me from the crowd.

They grew in my chest,
my mind, my soul,
until they began
to take shape, take hold.

You see, creation's not gentle,
it demands all,
your body, your mind,
your heart when it calls.

It asks for your time,
until you feel spent,
and still, you keep giving,
without consent.

For something inside you
refuses to rest,
it says love must be made,
not merely expressed.

I didn't just write,
I raised them with care,
taught them to speak,
to stumble, to dare.

To hold light in darkness,
to break, not fall,
every word shared,
a breath through it all.

As they grew stronger,
I grew aware,
like a parent who watches,
but cannot compare.

Now they've left me,
their journey begun,
wandering free
in the light of the sun.

And you, dear reader,
are where they now roam,
a world so vast,
they've found their new home.

And though I let go,
my heart holds tight,
afraid they'll be lost
in the vastness of night.

What if you see them
through eyes that don't know?

*What if they falter,
or stumble, or grow slow?*

*What if they wander,
forgetting my way,
the lessons I whispered,
the words I would say?*

*What if, in loving them,
you take them far,
and I can no longer
be where they are?*

Yet I know, deep inside,
it's the way they must go,
to leave me behind,
to wander, to grow.

Creation is letting go,
trusting the flow,
to nurture, then release,
its quiet woe.

Still, I hope when you
hold them with care,
you'll treat them as something
precious and rare.

For they carry traces
of who I am still,
my breath in the pauses,
my heart in the will.

If you find a thought,
a wound, or a spark,
a piece of your soul in
the words that embark,

Keep it with you,
that's all I desired,
for my words to live,
for my soul to be inspired.

And when the page closes
and you walk away,
know that in silence,
I'll feel you today.

The invisible thread
that ties us tight,
the quiet connection,
the shared light.

Because even once

they're far from my hand,
they're still mine, and yours,
as we both understand.

So thank you,
for holding them close,
for letting them fly,
for giving them life,
for watching them try.

Be kind to them,
and they will remember,
the hands that set them free,
and the soul that stays forever.

www.ingramcontent.com/pod-product-compliance
Lightning Source LLC
Chambersburg PA
CBHW060348050426
42449CB00011B/2866